I Wish...

I Wish...

Viktor Zubin

I Wish...

Copyright © 2023 by Viktor Zubin. All rights reserved.

No part of this publication may be reproduced, stored in a retrieval system or transmitted in any way by any means, electronic, mechanical, photocopy, recording or otherwise without the prior permission of the author except as provided by USA copyright law.

The opinions expressed by the author are not necessarily those of URLink Print and Media.

1603 Capitol Ave., Suite 310 Cheyenne, Wyoming USA 82001
1-888-980-6523 | admin@urlinkpublishing.com

URLink Print and Media is committed to excellence in the publishing industry.

Book design copyright © 2023 by URLink Print and Media. All rights reserved.

Published in the United States of America

Library of Congress Control Number: 2023921315
ISBN 978-1-68486-584-0 (Paperback)
ISBN 978-1-68486-585-7 (Digital)

02.11.23

Inspired By: Bruno Mars' *When I was your man*. All credit belongs to him.

Prologue

December 10, 2010

Mark was sitting at his desk in the living room, staring at a wedding invitation on the table. His eyes, originally brown in color, were now lifeless.

The invitation said, "You are invited to celebrate Arthur and Lola's union. Celebrate with them as they start a new chapter in their lives. The wedding ceremony is on December 10th at 12 pm. The wedding reception starts at 2 pm at the chapel".

On the cover of the wedding invite was a picture of a couple smiling. The man on the left was tall and handsome in a suit and a tie with blond hair. The woman on the right was very beautiful. She was wearing a purple dress which complemented nicely with her long black hair. The woman had a nice figure which made her look even more alluring.

Mark wasn't bad looking either, but due to neglect of physical fitness, he has lost most of his form and gained extra weight. After contemplating for a while, Mark decided to go to the wedding regardless of the consequences that might occur. Mark looked at the clock in the living room that showed 11: 45 am. With renewed vigor and determination Mark hurried out the front door to make it on time to the wedding ceremony.

Chapter

1

Chance Meeting

Disclaimer! Mark's point of view

December 31, 2008

I am sitting in church, listening to a sermon. Church service started at 7 pm. It's almost 8 already, 30 more minutes and we are free to go. The congregation itself is small. Not surprising, considering the overall population is below 1,000 people. Everybody knows everybody which means, if there is someone new, then everybody will know about it. I myself have been here a while, so I am not new.

After the church service concluded, everyone rushed out of the chapel to put the finishing touches on the New Year's feast. I was about to head home when I noticed a woman, who seemed lost. That is the sign of someone new. I guess everyone was in such a rush to get home that no one noticed her. I walked up to her, and asked, "Miss, may I help you?"

"Huh, yes please! You see sir, I am brand new here, I don't know anybody worse yet, I don't even have a place to spend the night."

"I could tell, say where are you from anyway?"

"Ah, it's a long story I don't want to bore you with it"

"You don't have to tell me, if you don't want to. Hey listen, I know this is a bit straightforward but, how about you come over to my place and we celebrate New Year's together, what do you say?"

"Are you sure it's alright? I wouldn't want to impose."

"It's fine, I live alone anyway so it doesn't matter"

"Oh, I trust you will not do anything indecent to this woman?"

"I wouldn't dare. I don't want to be the main topic of gossip"

"Alright then. I trust you"

"Welcome to my humble abode. My name's Mark by the way, what about you?"

"My name's Lola. It's nice to officially meet you." Lola extended her hand to me, looking for a handshake. I obliged her and apologized to her, "I am sorry, I know this little house is not much, but it's all I have."

"It's fine, don't worry about it. Thank you for taking me in."

"Don't mention it. It's my pleasure to shelter a beauty of your caliber.

Allow me to help you with your coat."

"Thank…you" Lola didn't expect to be complimented so nonchalantly. She even stuttered a little. She could feel the blood rushing to her cheeks. I helped Lola with her coat, and invited her to the dining table in the kitchen.

The house itself was small. Besides the kitchen, there was the living room with a desk and a chair with the clock on the wall. Lastly there was a bedroom and a single bathroom with a bathtub.

During dinner we talked a lot. So much so that we forgot about the passage of time. Before we knew it, it was already almost 12 am. One thing is for certain. I don't want to see this woman go. I liked talking to her plus she is drop dead gorgeous. She has black hair that falls down to her waist with an alluring figure to boot. In addition her lips are scarlet which only adds to her charm.

At that moment I said to myself, *If I don't make this woman my wife, then I will be the biggest dumbass on planet Earth!* With determination and resolve I asked Lola, "Did you know that there's a tradition that says that couples are supposed to kiss each other at midnight?"

"No, I have never heard of such a thing. Is it something new?"

"No, it's an old custom where, generally speaking, the couple who kiss at midnight tend to stay together forever. What do you say, want to give it a try? It's already midnight."

"If a kiss is all you require I am happy to oblique. I mean I have to show my gratitude somehow right?"

"Fine by me." *What have I done! I didn't think she would actually fall for that hook line and sinker! What do I do now? Get a hold of yourself Mark. All you have to do is kiss this drop-dead-gorgeous woman. Pretend like you have done this before. Here it goes.*

We both got up from the dining table. We got closer to each other. Our faces are inches apart at this point. I leaned in and kissed her. I couldn't wait any longer.

Chapter

2

Heartbroken

Disclaimer! Mark's point of view

March 8th, 2009

"We gather here today to celebrate the union of Mark and Lola. May they be blessed by God, and serve each other to the best of their abilities. By the power vested in me, I now pronounce you husband and wife. Mark, you may kiss your bride!"

I did as I was told and kissed Lola with all the passion I could muster. *Finally! I succeeded! I got the most beautiful woman in the world to marry me! Now I can die happy! I still can't believe that it all started with a kiss on New Year's Eve. The most amazing part? She answered me back! I didn't expect that!*

January 1, 2009 12:00 a.m.

"Will you marry me!"

"WHAAAAAAAAT! We barely know each other and you want me to marry you?"

"I am sorry, I know it's a bit sudden, but I realized that if I don't marry you, then I will regret it for the rest of my life!" Hearing what I had to say,

Lola blushed crimson red. "How can you say something so serious with a straight face? Do you even love me?"

"Of course I love you, I fell in love with you the moment I laid my eyes on you!" At this point I was blushing as well, it was embarrassing after all. In addition, I have never confessed my feelings like this before. I have no idea if this will actually work or not.

Lola blushed once again. Then she said, "I will marry you, but the both of us have to say the traditional vows to each other. Only under this condition will I marry you. I hope you will take care of me. Do you know what the traditional vows are?"

"Of course I do. They are: I take you, Lola, as my lawfully wedded wife, to have and to hold, from this day forward; for better, for worse, for richer, for poorer, in sickness and in health to love and to cherish till death do us part, so help me God this is my solemn vow"

Lola blushed once again. Once I realized what I said, I blushed as well. Then Lola repeated the vows back to me. Afterwards we stood there silently for a while staring at each other. Finally we jumped into each other's arms and kissed again, with more passion than ever before.

September 8, 2009 6:00 pm

"Honey, will you please pass the salt?"

"Hpm, take it yourself. It's right in the middle of the table"

"Lola, please don't start this, please?"

"I AM NOT STARTING ANYTHING!"

"WHAT IS YOUR PROBLEM!" At this point I am frustrated and angry we are both yelling at each other, while standing

"You want to know what my problem is? I made a mistake by marrying you! When was the last time we were on a date? I am not even mentioning a bouquet of flowers, or simple hand-holding. I have asked you many times to learn how to ballroom dance, so that we can dance together, but would you do it? No, you kept insisting that you will, 'learn it later'. Well guess what? I AM TIRED OF WAITING! Six months is enough!"

"ENOUGH!" I hit my fist on the table. The table shakes. "WILL YOU SHUT UP ALREADY! I am sick and tired of listening to your nagging! Going to parties and dancing is all you think about! In the last six months, when was the last time we made love to each other, huh?"

"Love-making? Don't make me laugh" Lola laughs loudly. "My heart has grown cold and resentful towards you. In fact, my love for you is negative. How could I let you touch me after you ignored me more than once? You know what? I AM DONE! Don't wait for me. Not now, not ever!" With those words Lola stormed out of our home. I never saw her again.

Chapter
3

Knight in Shining Armor

Disclaimer! Arthur's point of view

September 8, 2009 10:00 pm

My life is over. My wife has filed for divorce. My reputation is ruined. I don't know what happened. Most likely, my wife held a grudge against me for many years. That's understandable. I mean, we have been married for almost five years now. However, I still don't understand what caused my wife to "explode" all of a sudden. There were no warning signs at all(I think). Well, whatever. It doesn't matter anymore. No matter what I say or do she won't believe me anymore.

With those thoughts I entered the local bar. I was a regular there, so most of the guys knew me. I sat at the counter. The bartender is an old buddy of mine, so he often gave me discounts and was a nice guy to talk to. I ordered my regular drink. I wanted to get drunk to forget my worries, at least for a while. An hour later, a lady stormed into the bar. She was an absolute beauty. However, she was furious.

"Barkeep! Please get me scotch on the rocks!"

The bartender looked at the lady and said quizzingly, "Miss, are you sure you're able to afford it?"

Instead of the lady I answered, "Put it on my tab". The bartender seeing the look in my eyes understood me completely. He came up to me and whispered, "Good luck". He continued his duties with a smile. The lady sat down next to me, "Thank you" she whispered and sighed deeply.

"A hard day?"

"Yea"

"Would you care to share your worries with me?"

The woman eyed me suspiciously at first then said nonchalantly, "My husband is an asshole"

I burst in laughter, spilling some of my drink that was in my mouth. She gets angry at me and says, "What was so funny?" She pouted and folded her arms across her chest.

"I am sorry, I didn't mean to laugh. It's just that your answer was not something that I was expecting."

"What were you expecting?"

"I thought you would put on a facade of 'everything is fine', but you didn't. It's kind of refreshing honestly."

"Yea well, six months of pretending to be happy is enough for me My name's Lola by the way" She extended her hand

I took to shake it, "Arthur"

"Here you go Miss, one scotch on the rocks" The bartender came back and brought Lola her drink.

"Thank you"

After that, we talked a lot. Lola told me about husband, Mark, how he refused to change and forgot the basics with which to keep a woman in love with you. I in turn, told Lola my struggles and marriage problems. My wife Katty, is the quiet type. She only says something when she's on the verge of "exploding". I told her many times that, if she wants something from me, then she should say so in a straight-forward manner. However, she didn't listen. She said, "If you really loved me, then I shouldn't have to tell you what I want!" What kind of a delusion is that! Following that logic, my boss at work should know that I want a promotion and should just give it to me without me saying so. Ridiculous.

"Hey, are you alright?" Lola looked at me worriedly

"What? Oh, I'm fine. I got lost in my thoughts there for a second. Say Lola, did you know that you are very pretty? That husband of yours is an idiot for letting such a beautiful creature like yourself slip right through his fingers"

"I will take that as a compliment" I noticed that Lola's face was red.

However, I couldn't tell if she was blushing or drunk. Most likely both.

"Say Lola, is it just me or is it getting hot in here? Would you want to go somewhere more comfortable?"

"Sure why not" Lola answered in her drunken state, "Did you know that I didn't have sex with my husband for almost half a year? I did it on purpose too, he wasn't treating me right"

"You don't say" I scratched my chin as if contemplating something important. "Let me take you to an inn. It's not far from here"

"Alright"

"Ben, buddy thanks for everything" I stumbled on my two feet trying to find balance. Lola while trying to help me stumbled as well. After a while we were able to lock shoulder-to-shoulder and stumbled our way out of the bar. Ben, the bartender, was left alone to tend to the bar. "Arthur you lucky bastard" he mumbled with a smirk on his face

When Lola and I stumbled into the only inn in this town. There was a receptionist by the name Jenny. She recognized Lola right away and was speechless. "Lola, is that you? What the hell happened to you? Have you been drinking? Who's this man next to you?" I got sick of her questions and said in an irritated tone, "Lady please give us a room I will pay for it"

Jenny was shocked even more so, "I AM NOT GIVING YOU A ROOM! YOU'RE GONNA DEFILE LOLA!" At this point I was extremely angry. I said, "Who are you to teach me what I should or should not be doing? Give me the key to one of the rooms or I WILL KILL YOU!" I sobered up for a moment and looked Jenny in the eyes with murderous intent.

Jenny was terrified. Her whole body was shaking. She hurriedly took out one of the keys and handed it to me. "The first room on the right" Lola and I stumbled our way into the room, and closed the door on a lock.

Jenny was so terrified, she ran onto the streets to look for the police, leaving the inn behind. If she would have stayed, then she would have heard the sound of pleasure and moans that echoed throughout the inn.

Chapter

4

Memories and Regret

Disclaimer! Mark's point of view

Jenny ran onto the streets and called out for help. "Please somebody help!" One of the policemen on duty heard her and called out to her, "What is it Miss?"

"Please you gotta help me" she begged "my friend she's about to be taken advantage of by a man"

"What kind of condition were they in?"

"They were both staggering, hanging on to each other for support, most likely drunk."

"Listen lady, what you described is a common occurrence. Most likely here is what happened: people met at a bar, got drunk, and now are having sex at the inn. People make their own choices"

"If what you say is true then you gotta help all the more. My friend, she is already married and she is having sex with somebody to whom she is not married."

"That sounds like a family problem to me. Maybe the husband should have been paying more attention to his wife" Dejected Jenny chose to return to the inn.

Once at the inn she heard the sounds of pleasure and moans that echoed through the inn. She followed the sounds and was shocked by what she saw

She left me! Can you believe it? She left me! Why did she leave me? Everything was going great
"Flashbacks"

"Honey, will you please take me out on a date? We haven't been on a date in a while. If you do it I will have a surprise for you later"(Smirk knowingly)
"Babe, I would love to. I really would, but I have work. It's a big project that cannot be delayed. Sorry"
"Again? That's what you said last time! So, you really can't afford to take your wife? Fine be that way! Hpm!"(Left angrily while pouting)
"Honey, I signed us up for ballroom dancing lessons. Are you coming?"
"Why didn't you tell me anything ahead of time?"
"I did, you just don't listen!"
"Go on without me. I am going to the sauna with Ben. Besides, I can learn how to ballroom dance later"
"Alright fine, but next time you're coming with me right?"
"Yea yea yea. Next time"
(I never went with her even once)

"Honey, there is a party at Jenny's this Saturday, we are going right?"
"Go to the party without me. I am too tired from work. I will stay at home and rest"

"You never go anywhere with me! Fine, stay at home if you wish, I am going by myself!"(Leaves angry and resentful).

I have lost count of how many fights we have had in the last six months. I was a terrible husband! Oh, God what have I done? No wonder she left me! What should I do? I know I will get Lola back and beg for her forgiveness!

"Knock Knock"

There was a knock on the door. I opened the door. In front of me stood a tall man in a business suit

"Hello, how may I help you?"

"Are you Mark?"

"Yes, I am. What seems to be the issue sir."

"My name is Michael. I was hired by your wife Lola. I have divorce papers that require your signature."

Chapter

5

Game over!

Disclaimer! Mark's point of view

"Divorce papers? What do you mean by 'divorce papers'?"

"I mean what I said. Your wife wants a divorce Mark."

"But why?" At this point I was confused, frustrated, angry perhaps.

The question most likely geared at myself more than anybody else.

"I don't know Mark. It's none of my business. However, according to your wife and I quote, 'He treated me horribly. Never wanting to participate in my favorite activities. He never seems to have the time for me, even when I asked him multiple times for attention he doesn't budge.'"

"I agree that I was far from the best husband I could have been for my wife. However, those things that she described are all fixable. Go tell Lola that I beg for her forgiveness and ask her to come home."

"Mark, I am glad that you have realized your mistakes and I will tell your words to your wife. However, most likely, your wife doesn't want anything to do with you at this point."

"Are you telling me that the only way I will be able to see my wife again is through court?"

"That is precisely what I am saying. You have lost your chance Mark.

I am sorry."

"Michael, will you please tell my wife that I love her, please. I used to say it to her all the time. But then I got caught up in work and forgot to pay attention to my wife."

"Don't worry my friend, I will tell her what you said, word for word" "Thank you. See you in court. I will make things right this time".

With determination in my eyes, I prepared myself to face my wife once again, but this time in court.

(Arthur's house)

"Honey, I'm home!" Katty came through the front door with a bag of groceries. She went to the kitchen to put the groceries away. That's when she heard moaning sounds coming from the Master Bedroom. She followed the sounds to the bedroom and discovered her husband in their bed with another woman.

Arthur felt the gaze of his wife. Then he panicked and said, "Babe, it's not what it looks like. I can explain!" With shock and tears in her eyes she ran out of the room. Meanwhile, the woman covered herself and started to get dressed after Katty left the room.

Arthur was trying his best to stop his wife from leaving the house. However, before he got the chance to explain himself, there was a knock on the door. Arthur, now fully dressed, answered the door.

"Hey Michael, how are you? Did you find anything? Good news?"

"Yes, I did find a man called Mark. I gotta say, he regrets what he has done and is asking Lola, his wife, to forgive him." Lola, of course, didn't hear any of this.

"Huh, he finally understands now. Too bad, his wife is already mine".

When Katty heard this, she started sobbing even harder than before.

"He didn't sign the divorce papers. He wants to go to court"

"If he wants to go to court, it's fine by me" At this time Lola came out of the bedroom full clothed and make-up on.

"What did I miss?"

(The court house)

Everyone in attendance was familiar with one-another. That's why, it came as a shock to everyone present that Lola and I were getting divorced.

"Court is in session!" said the judge. I stood on one side while Lola stood on the other. "Lola, I want to apologize to you for being a horrible husband. Please forgive me. I heard that you were the one who filed for the divorce papers. Is that true? Tell me it isn't true"

"It's true! I was the one who filed for the divorce, so what? I was tired of waiting for you to finally have some time for me in your busy schedule.

That's why I did it. Are you mad now?"

"No, just disappointed…in myself. I should have gone on those dates you wanted to go on. I should have; given you flowers or held your hand in public but I didn't. I am truly sorry."

"I don't need your apology anymore! You know why? I don't care about you anymore! I have Arthur now."

"Arthur, who is Arthur?"

"Someone whom you will never be."

I was hurt by her words, but I tried not to let it show. I continued to persuade her saying, "I know that you're mad at me and you have every right to be mad at me. The only reason you fell into Arthur's arms is because I neglected my duties and responsibilities as your husband.

Please come back home and let's start over"

"You weren't listening were you. I don't care about you or what you have to say. I am not coming home with you. I have a new home now, together with Arthur." While Lola and I were talking back and forth, there was sobbing in the background. Katty was sobbing heavily, almost to the point of losing control of herself.

The judge, seeing that Lola is set on getting a divorce, despite my persuasion attempts, finalized our divorce according to Lola's wishes. I dejectedly left the court house.

January 1st 2010 12:00 pm.

It is New Year's. I am celebrating it by myself for the first time. It's been almost a year since Lola and I got divorced. To be honest I still cannot get over her. I constantly reminisce about what happened and I blame myself constantly. I am at the point now where I don't know what to do with my life.

Over time I gained some weight. Became even more depressed because of my weight and I wanted to die. My eyes lost their color and became lifeless.

Ben would sometimes come over to try to cheer me up but to no avail. I couldn't forget about Lola.

December 10, 2010

It's been almost two years since the divorce with Lola. My health, both physical and mental, became worse. It's as if something inside me snapped and I couldn't handle it properly.

Suddenly there was a knock on the door. I opened the door and in front of me stood Jenny. "Lola wanted you to have this." saying that Jenny disappeared just as fast as she had appeared. I didn't even have time to ask any questions. I closed the door with a confused look on my face.

In my hand I held an envelope. However, when I opened the envelope, I was shocked by what I found inside.

Epilogue

Disclaimer! Mark's point of view

I drove as fast as I could to the chapel where Lola and I first got married. Once I got there, I dashed inside. Thankfully I was not late. There's five minutes remaining until the beginning of the wedding ceremony.

"Do you Arthur, take Lola to be your lawfully wedded wife?"
"I do!"
"Do you Lola, take Arthur to be your lawfully wedded husband?"
"I do!"
"Please say the traditional wedding vows."

Both Arthur and Lola said their vows one after the other. When I heard the vows. My heart ached. *How could Lola so easily repeat the same vows to another man?*

With a deep sigh I continued to watch the ceremony. Once the ceremony concluded, I went outside to get some fresh air. Thankfully no one came up to me. Maybe they felt pity for me, for literally being replaced by another, but I didn't really care.

Then came the time of the feast. Everyone who was invited ate their fill, me included. When it came time to give a present to the bride and the groom, I didn't give them anything. I didn't have anything to give. My now ex-wife took everything in the divorce settlement. All I was left with was the car that I drove in.

After the gift giving, came the wish making segment of the feast. Everyone was supposed to say something that was on their hearts or minds. One person sang a solo. Then there was a trio that sang another song. Finally there was a person who read a verse as s wish to the married couple.

After that there was the ballroom dancing segment. When many couples started to ballroom dance my heart ached again inside of me. *This was the dance that Lola wanted to dance with me and I refused her!* I thought to myself. At this point, the bride and groom were right in the middle of the dance floor. I mustered up the courage and walked out onto the stage. Some were surprised, to say the least, to see me walking up, while others were curious as to what I was going to do.

"If you don't mind, I would like to sing a song dedicated to the bride"

With that I started to sing(piano starts to play. At the same time, the married couples started twirling in circles with each other).

I Wish...

Same bed, but it feels just a little bit bigger now
Our song on the radio, but it don't sound the same
When our friends talk about you, All it does is just tear me down
'Cause my heart breaks a little when I hear your name

// Chorus //
It all just sounds like oooooh ooh
Mmm, too young, too dumb to realize
That I should have bought you flowers
And held your hand
Should have gave you all my hours when I had the chance
Take you to every party,
'Cause all you wanted to do was dance
Now my baby's dancing,
But she's dancing with another man

My pride, my ego, my needs,
And my selfish ways
Caused a good, strong woman like you
To walk out my life
Now I'll never, never get to clean up
The mess I made, oh
And it haunts me every time I
close my eyes

It all just sounds like oooooh ooh
Mmm, too young, too dumb to realize
That I should have bought you flowers
And held your hand
Should have gave you all my hours when I had the chance
Take you to every party,
'Cause all you wanted to do was dance Now my baby's dancing,
But she's dancing with another man

Although it hurts, I'll be the first
To say that I was wrong
Oh, I know I'm probably much too late,
To try and apologize for my mistakes
But I just want you to know

I hope he buys you flowers,
I hope he holds your hand
Give you all his hours,
When he has the chance

Take you to every party,
'Cause I remember how much you
loved to dance
Do All the things I should have done, When I
was your man

Do All the things I should have done, When I
was your man

(Piano stops playing, thunderous applause follow)

When I finished singing, everyone applauded with standing ovations. I bowed a little bow and proceeded to step down from the stage. Seeing that I said everything I wanted to say to Lola in the song, I headed towards the exit.

I noticed that many women had tears coming down their faces, while others were teary-eyed. I guess the song struck them somehow.

I got into my car and headed home. At that moment[on my way home]I caught myself smiling in the mirror.

Bonus Chapter

My Miserable Life

Disclaimer! Lola's point of view

December 31, 2008

I came to the chapel because I didn't know where to go. I was brand-new in town, so I didn't know what's what. I don't know if it was luck or not, but that night I met Mark.

He was a nice guy, who tried to help me the best he could. He asked me questions and then invited me to his place to celebrate the coming of the New Year. I was skeptical and nervous, especially after he mentioned that he lived alone

However, after he assured me that won't try anything weird since he doesn't want rumors to spread, we walked to his home. The house was relatively small. It had a; kitchen, a living room with a desk and a clock on the wall right down the middle. Finally, there was the bedroom with a nightstand.

After we had dinner, it was almost 12 am. Mark asked me to marry him. At first I was confused, then shock followed soon afterward. Then Mark started to explain. In short, he said that I am the most beautiful woman he has ever seen. He added that if he didn't have me as his wife, then he will regret it forever.

I know it sounds corny but I believed him. Clearly I am a beautiful woman, and I would be lying if I said that I wasn't attracted to him also. Mark had a nice physique and a handsome face with brown eyes. Before I knew it, Mark and I were kissing when the clock struck midnight.

March 8, 2009

Today is my wedding day. I am the happiest woman alive. Both of us exchanged our vows. Mark looked dazzling. I couldn't stop blushing because Mark would stare so intently at me in my wedding dress I didn't know what to think. On one hand I was happy that he had such passion towards me, on the other hand I was worried that I wouldn't be able to handle his passion.

Our first month as a married couple passed in a flash. I felt as if I was in heaven. We would play with each other. All kinds of games. My three favorites were; Hide 'n' Seek, Musical chairs, and a game called "Palms"(A two player game where you put your palms together, and repeat a sequence. With each successful repetition of the sequence, increase the speed until one of you fails). The reason why they were my favorites is because, no matter the outcome, we would always kiss at the end. This in turn would often lead to a passionate lovemaking session ☺

However, our happiness would not last long. From the second month onwards Mark started making excuses as to why he cannot do this or that. I would tell him that I want to go on a date, he says that he's too busy working. I tried multiple times. I even bartered with him saying that if he takes me out on a date, then I am his tonight. He ignored me. I started getting angry.

Another month went by, no action on his part at all. Then I decided to try again. Mark has promised me that he will attend ballroom dancing lessons with me that I signed us up for. Again he gave an excuse saying that he already made plans with Ben to go to a sauna. This time I was really mad. Not only did he break his promise to me, but he gave me another excuse as to why he could not attend. My resentment towards

Mark has started to grow Little by little my resentment towards Mark grew with each passing day. All because he wouldn't bring me flowers even though I asked for flowers on multiple occasions.

Finally my last straw broke. I heard that Jenny, my best friend, is having a party this upcoming Saturday. Mark and I were invited of course. But alas, Mark gave yet another excuse that he was tired. I was at my boiling point. "Fine stay, then!" I said and stormed out the door.

September 8 2009 6:00 pm

We were having, what seemed like a nice quiet dinner that is, until Mark asked me to pass him the salt. Now, the request itself is ordinary.

However at that moment, I was anything but calm. I still couldn't forget Mark's transgressions against me. Therefore, I angrily told him to get it himself.

Naturally, he didn't react well. He yelled at me, I yelled back at him. This seemed almost like a routine at this point. Both of us yelled at one another telling each other what the other one wanted the most. Our fight escalated from there. Finally I snapped and stormed out of the house, for good this time.

I was mad and hurt at the same time. All I could think of to lessen the pain was alcohol. It took me a while to find the local bar. By the time I got there, the bar was filled with regulars. I sat at the counter and ordered a scotch on the rocks. Next to me sat a gentleman, who introduced himself as Arthur.

Arthur was nice enough to pay for my scotch. Over the course of the evening, I found out that he and I have a lot in common. His wife doesn't understand him. My husband doesn't understand me. We shared everything. By the end of the night, both of us were drunk as a skunk. At this point Arthur offered to take me to an inn. I agreed.

When we stumbled our way into the inn. I didn't recognise the receptionist. Arthur got the inn key[by threatening the receptionist] and we made our way into the room. Arthur made love to me in that room. It was as if I was possessed. I didn't know where this ferocity came from. It was probably due to the fact that I wasn't touched by my husband in several months that I pounced at my "prey" like a hungry lioness.

After our "wild" night together, Arthur and I decided to move in together{to his house]. At the time I was unaware of the fact that his wife didn't know about me. I thought that has told his wife about me.With Arthur's help, I was able to hire an attorney by the name of Michael.

Michael was money well spent. He got all the necessary paperwork for a divorce settlement and went off to Mark so that he would sign the divorce papers. I signed the papers right away. I didn't want anything to do with Mark anymore.

To celebrate, we had a lavish lunch, followed by passionate love making. We were so captivated by each other that we didn't notice how Arthur's wife came in. Before we knew it, we were caught red-handed. I tried to cover myself to the best of my ability. Arthur ran after her, trying to explain himself.

Needless to say, she was devastated. She couldn't stop sobbing. All the groceries that she had brought were now on the bedroom floor. In the chaos, I took my time getting dressed and doing light make-up. By the time I got out of the bedroom, Arthur was already talking to Michaael, while his wife continued to sob, barely controlling herself.

Apparently, Mark refused to sign the divorce papers. If that's the case, then the only way out is through the court. In court, I was very surprised. Reason being, Mark has changed. I could tell because his tone of voice changed completely when addressing me.

He kept asking forgiveness and begging me to return to him. However, I would have none of it. *You've had your chance buddy, multiple in fact, but too bad for you I don't care anymore!* With those thoughts I pressed to get my divorce finalized. Seeing my restlessness and the fact that Mark's persuasion isn't working, the judge finally obliged. My divorce was finalized.

To my surprise, Arthur's wife filed for divorce also. *Finally! I didn't think she had the guts* I thought. Arthur's divorce was finalized fairly quickly. With Arthur's wife out of the way, I now have the chance to have Arthur all to myself. He proposed to me fairly quickly after his divorce was final. To rub it in to Mark's face, I sent him a wedding invitation and had Jenny deliver it for me

December 10, 2010

My wedding day. The funny thing is, both of my weddings were at the same chapel. I guess it's not that surprising considering the fact that the population of the town is small but still, the place left a bad taste in my mouth.

To my surprise, Mark actually came to the wedding ceremony. I was gloating. *Look Mark! How does it make you feel to see your wife stolen from you by another man? Serves you right! You should have treated me better!*

After the ceremony, came the wedding banquet. Everyone was enjoying their meal. All I could hear was the sound of metal on metal(spoons, forks and knives). After everyone was fed, came the gift giving segment. Many people gave us gifts.

After that came the wishing segment. People would sing songs or say a verse to wish something ro Arthur and I. After the wishing segment, came my favorite part – Ballroom dancing! Everyone who was married paired up started to twirl. Needless to say, Arthur and I were the center of attention.

Then something happened that I didn't expect. Mark got up on stage. He said that he would like to sing a song dedicated to the bride. Naturally people were curious. Mark started to sing. What surprised me the most were the song lyrics. The lyrics were basically describing my life with Mark!

However, what shocked me the most is, towards the end of the song, Mark was wishing for my new man to do all the things he couldn't do. He was talking to me through the song! At that point

I couldn't hold it in anymore. Tears were streaming down my face and there was no stopping them.

After Mark finished singing the song, everyone applauded with standing ovations[including me]. After that, Mark walked through the crowd in a hurry to leave. I noticed that someone was trying to follow him, but I paid no mind to it. I could care less about Mark, he was too late. Now I am looking forward to life with Arthur, my new husband.

Bonus Chapter

Devastation and Hope

Disclaimer! Katty's point of view

Arthur and I were married for almost five years. We got married in 2005. Everything was perfect, for about a year. My husband loved me and I loved him in return. Our love life was wonderful, better at some parts I would say. However, as the years went on, he showed up less and less at home. I was starting to suspect that he has a mistress on the side, but there was no evidence to support my claim.

Arthur would often visit the local bar. At first it used to be only on the weekends. However, as the years rolled by, his trip to the bar became more and more frequent. I didn't mind that he would go out drinking with his buddies on the weekends, but weekdays, that's too much. This dilemma of drinking often was the cause of countless arguments.

During our fourth year of marriage, I was told by a doctor that, most likely, I won't have children because I am not fertile. When I told my husband the news, he got mad at me and called me useless. I was extremely agitated and hurt by his words. *How am I useless? It's not my fault that I am unable to conceive with a child.* From that moment on, Arthur refused to touch me as a woman.

One day, when I came home with a bag of groceries, I heard moaning sounds coming from the master bedroom. When I saw my husband on top of another woman, I was shook to the core. Tears flowed down my face. I was shocked, angry and sad all in one. So much so that I dropped all the groceries, along with the bag, on the bedroom floor with my mouth wide open.

Arthur bolted off the woman and started making excuses like; "I can explain!", "She came onto me, it's not my fault!", "It's not what it looks like!", "Let's talk about this like adults", and many others. However, I would have none of it. I was about to let him have it, when there was a knock on the door.

Arthur went to open the door. Meanwhile, I was sobbing on the couch in our living room, still unable to accept the fact that my husband committed adultery. When Arthur came back, there was a man with him. Apparently, the man was hired by my husband to gather documents for a divorce settlement. As it turns out, the husband of that whore refused to sign the divorce papers, so the matter will have to be settled through court.

Naturally as Arthur's wife I had to be present to tell my side of the story. However, I was genuinely surprised by the attitude of the husband. Here I thought he would be as angry as can be, but no he was doing the complete opposite. He was asking for forgiveness and begging his wife to come back home.

At that moment I was jealous of the fact that my husband never asked me for forgiveness, yet this man is asking that bitch to forgive him. *If only I had a husband like him.* I thought to myself. However, I quickly shook my head to get the unnecessary thoughts out of my head.

The couple who were divorcing were Mark and Lola(I still prefer bitch or whore). Apparently, they had their own problems. I laughed at myself saying, "The grass looks greener on the other side"..However, I was still curious about Mark. What would cause a man to change so drastically?

A while later I filed for divorce. Now that my husband has that bitch, I didn't want anything to do with him. Thankfully, Arthur gave me what I wanted. Quick and easy. As soon as our divorce was finalized, Arthur proposed to that whore and started to prepare for his wedding.

I was given an ultimatum by Arthur, I had to find a place to live by the time Arthur gets married for the second time. Needless to say, I wasn't pleased.

December 10, 2010

During the wedding ceremony I was disgusted. I was disgusted by the fact that Arthur has the nerve to smile so innocently at that whore, while pretending as if nothing happened between us. *How could I have fallen in love with such a man?* I thought to myself, shuddering at the thought..

When it came time for the banquet, no matter how much I tried to eat, I couldn't. My life has basically gone to hell and back and I am supposed to smile? No way!

Next, came the gift giving segment. *Huh, you ain't getting nothing from me, bitch!* Then came the wishing well segment[to the newly wedded couple]. *How can I wish well upon someone who has destroyed my life as I know it? No thank you.* After that came the ballroom dancing. *Now that's depressing.*

I was so engrossed in my thoughts that I barely heard the sound of a man's voice on stage saying that he wants to sing a song dedicated to the bride. I was about to scold him in my mind, but as I lifted my head to see who the idiot was dedicating a song to that bitch, I was shocked beyond belief. It was Mark from the court trials.

I was utterly confused, why would he dedicate a song to his ex-wife. Then as Mark continued to sing, I gradually understood. Mark was using the song to talk to his wife one last time.

Before I knew it, I was crying like a little baby. Now the pieces started coming together. Most likely, Mark was the jerk in the relationship. As a result, his wife left him. During the time in which he was alone, he realized his mistakes, and tried to get his wife back. Unfortunately for him, his wife didn't care about him enough anymore to listen to what he has to say, hence the song.

The song was used as the ultimate apology. At this point, many people were teary-eyed and had tears running down their faces. By the time Mark finished the song, everyone applauded with standing ovations.

I, on the other hand, wanted to follow him, to talk to him. There he goes, coming down the stage. I tried to follow him, but I was slowed down by the crowd of people getting in my way. By the time I got out of the chapel, Mark was already in his car driving away. All I could see was the silhouette of the car in the distance, getting further and further away from me.

All I could do was throw my hands up in the air in frustration. Left with no other choice, I went back inside the chapel reluctantly. As I walked inside, I promised myself to find Mark and talk to him. Will I find Mark? Only time will tell.

Afterword

Thank you for purchasing another one of my works. Did you like it? Even if you didn't please provide me with honest feedback, it doesn't matter if it's positive or negative. If you didn't like it tell me why and what you would do to change it or make it better. You can do this by leaving a review on the online stores(like Amazon or Barnes & Noble).

I am not planning to continue the story. However, if you have a good story idea then you can email it to me at zubinviktor@yahoo.com. Please put your idea in the subject headline and then describe your idea. Make sure to have a starting point and an endpoint.

As far as future plans go, I am going to write a book called, "I loved you, you never loved me" Stay tuned.

Finally, thank you Dorrance Publishing for putting in the time and the effort to make this book possible. I hope we can continue working together

www.ingramcontent.com/pod-product-compliance
Lightning Source LLC
LaVergne TN
LVHW021741060526
838200LV00052B/3396